"Dad died today"

"Dad died today"

A pocket guide to childhood grief

Jack Mallory

Every Cloud

Copyright © 2023 by Jack Mallory

All rights reserved. No part of this book may be reproduced in any manner whatsoever without written permission except in the case of brief quotations embodied in critical articles and reviews.

First Printing, 2023

To all of those who feel lost in their own grief but must prevail to help others. Bless you all.

CONTENTS

DEDICATION v

1 Introduction 1

2 Grief and Mourning 12

3 Changes in the Family Dynamic 17

4 Guilt and Blame 20

5 Support Systems 23

6 Coping Mechanisms 28

7 Long Term Effects 32

CONTENTS

8 | The Reality of Loss 40

9 | My Advice 44

ABOUT THE AUTHOR 51
OTHER BOOKS BY THIS AUTHOR
53

Introduction

This is a guide, which, sadly, I was destined to write, for I lost my 44 year old father to cancer when I was 18 years old, which at the time of writing is 42 years ago. Now, reading that statement you may be thinking that I wasn't really a child, but as an 18 year old you are on the cusp of being both a child and an adult. In my case I had watched my Dad slowly waste away from this terrible disease for nearly 2 years before he finally succumbed to it.

In a nutshell my intention for this book is for it to be a self-help guide for both children and adults on how to cope with the loss of a loved one. This book will provide insight into the grieving process, as well as tips on how to cope with the challenges associated with childhood bereavement.

It all began for me when I had just turned 16. My Dad had been sent home from work after being discovered sitting in a corner shaking uncontrollably. He thought he had some sort of bug and, after a doctor's appointment, he was relieved to have been told that it was just a stomach upset. I had never seen my Dad unwell before so was naturally worried and felt a feeling of what I can only describe as dread. Needless to say he became progressively unwell, losing weight rapidly and his skin turning yellow. There were several diagnoses given over the next few months including jaundice and gout, but eventually he was referred to a specialist, who promptly sent him for a biopsy operation. The biopsy revealed that my Dad had a Tumour on his liver. Strangely the word tumour did not ring any alarm bells that it meant cancer, despite the fact that really they are one and the same; so we were a little more positive about things now. My Dad, however, was not allowed to return to work so ended up on what was called an

Invalidity Pension. Being a proud man who had been a professional soldier for the first 24 working years of his life, he was devastated. His condition did not improve, he couldn't keep any food down, and he literally became a walking skeleton, was basically bed ridden, rarely being able to venture downstairs. I recall vividly my Grandad visiting and asking my Mum about the prognosis. None of my other siblings were around at the time and I remember her tearfully blurting out that he wasn't "going to survive", but at the same time insisting that she didn't want him to know.

Although my personal trauma had already begun, this secret that I now had to keep, from the father who I loved, and the rest of my family, really broke me; and my grief had already commenced. I was sixteen and spent the next year hoping and praying that my Dad would get better. When I look back at it now it was a hell of a thing to carry and not be able to tell anyone. That said, my best friend at school asked me how my Dad was doing and I felt the need to tell someone, so I chose him. Nothing dramatic, for I could not even say the words, so I basically repeated what my Mum had said. I think my friend was stunned and, to be honest, we never spoke of it again, but I felt a little better having shared it. Life carried on as normal for me. In my spare time I was in the Air Force Cadets. Apart from school that was my only outlet from the continual thoughts, fear and praying. Cancer likes to play tricks on your heart, for my Dad would have periods where he went back to normal, gained weight and was himself, but then he would sink back to being ill, as fast as he had apparently recovered. These ups and downs made me feel that my prayers *were* being answered.

I truly believe in his heart that my Dad knew he wasn't going to recover, but he never said anything, and was always positive. I remember sitting on his bed and having a chat with him. I had always wanted to be a soldier like him, and he was giving me all sorts of advice and telling me that when I complete my basic training it was his intention to come to the parade in a hired Rolls Royce. I felt so proud and happy at that moment. Christmas 1980 was one of the times of what you would probably call remission for him, but I think he knew that this would be his last one. My Dad, like me, loved

"DAD DIED TODAY"

Christmas, and always made sure we had loads of presents. Despite their lack of money, this Christmas was no different; in fact he made sure we had everything we needed, great food, presents and plenty of laughter. My Dad had a cheeky sense of humour which I have inherited and we laughed at silly things, not caring what other people thought. As the months came and went, so did his health and this time there was no coming back. He was thin, yellow, and gaunt, his legs had swelled so much that his skin had split, and he could hardly walk. I still prayed to myself, but felt useless and abandoned by the God whom I had spoken to all of my life. My Dad had never been a fan of Fathers Day so never celebrated it or expected anything, but this year I felt the need to at least buy him a card. My Dad had a big nose and, remembering a line from a Monty Python film, I wrote in the card "Happy Fathers Day Conk Face". Again my father was bedridden but when I gave him the card on the Friday before Fathers Day he opened it and had a good chuckle about it. To this day I don't know why I gave him the card on the Friday, but I felt drawn to do so, just to tell him how much I loved him. All I could say is that it must have been fate because he died the following morning, Saturday 20th June 1981; a date now etched forever more on my mind. The saddest thing is that my Dad died alone. My 2 sisters had left home, my brother was watching morning television, whilst my Mum was at the launderctte. I was at my friend's house that morning helping him turn a cellar in to a work shop of sorts, but I remember before I left, hearing my dad talking in his sleep. I stepped in to the bedroom and saw him tossing and turning and saying "pick me up, pick me up". I wonder to this day if he was seeing the light and asking the Angels to take him with them, away from his pain. I hope so.

That morning was the beginning of great sadness and pain, but also one of awe. As I have already mentioned, I was at my friend's house, which was probably about 5 miles away. At around 11am my 13 year old brother arrived, having ridden there on his bike. I asked him why he was there and he simply said "Dad died today", then cycled back home. What a brave thing for a young boy to do and say. It took me years to be able to say any words which even resembled those, so I have always been in awe of that little boy and have never forgotten that moment, hence the title of this book. Another thing I recall is my friend putting his hand on my shoulder and me pulling away. I didn't want anyone feeling sorry for me, but I remember saying "what's my Mum going to do now?"

When I got home I found that the house was full of relatives who we hardly saw. I have to say, I did feel a little angry, but obviously they were there for my Mum, so I do appreciate that. I went in to the living room. I think I gave my Mum a hug. I went to sit down but didn't quite get there before I burst in to tears and ran upstairs. I lay on my bed all day crying and didn't come down until the relatives had left. I just could not face them or what I deemed as their almost expected concern and offers of "if there is anything I can do...."

Both my parents had had a hard upbringing and as a result there were never any hugs or kisses; not that I don't think they loved us, because they did, they just didn't express it. Death is a strange thing because although I didn't want my Dad to die, when it happened it was almost a relief, mainly for him to be pain free, but also for me not having to wake every day worrying for him and constantly praying. It sounds terrible I know, and I have felt that guilt ever since. I think the worst thing for me about the whole saga is that once my dad *had* died there was no support from each other, no hugs, and certainly nothing from the relatives who had offered it. Basically, my Dad was rarely spoken of again, as if he had never existed. He was gone. The relief of no more pain or worry was there, and that was it.

There was, however, one final trauma to experience, and that was my first funeral. One thing that I have mixed feelings about is that my mother made my brother and I go with her to the funeral home to view my Dad in his coffin. He was the first dead person I had ever seen. He looked peaceful, and he looked like the man I had always loved. His hands were crossed and linked by their thumbs and my Mum placed his Fathers Day cards and condolence cards across his chest, to be cremated with him. I'm glad that she did that as I felt that my words of love were with him forever. Strangely enough one thing that has stuck with me is that he had about 5 whiskers on his chin. I remember saying that they hadn't shaved him, but maybe your body still continues doing a few things when you are gone. I don't know. Although I didn't really want to be there, I wish now that I could have had a private moment to say a few personal words to him and to give him a goodbye kiss. But it didn't happen.

The funeral itself was a nightmare for me personally. I did not cry and felt that I couldn't show any emotion. I remember when the hearse arrived at our house there were nosey neighbours, who we didn't even know, congregating and staring. I just thought, "how dare you?" and brought my hand up to my eyes in the shape of binoculars as if to say "what are you looking at?" The funeral was at a crematorium so it meant that we didn't have to do it twice and go and stand around an open grave. Thank goodness. There were a lot of people there, but few who I knew because my Dad's time in the Army meant that we did not know our relatives. I remember the Vicar, who like most, did not know my Dad, so spoke of him from what he had been told. The man could not pronounce the letter R which made me chuckle to myself for I knew that it was something which would have appealed to my Dad's funny side. At the end of the service I sat and watched as the coffin descended out of sight on some sort of lift/elevator. At that moment I stood up and walked out the chapel. It was all I could do to stop myself crying.

And that was it. Life carried on as normal. No one spoke of my Dad. I told none of my friends of his death. It took me years to even say the words, and even then I would have trouble getting them out without tearing up. It has indeed been a traumatic time for me and still is. I have never got over it, but have learned to live with it. But would it have been different if I had been able to speak of it with someone or even had a family who showed some sign of wanting to help each other? Probably; but I will never know. But this is why I have written this guide, so that you can have an insight and hopefully help a child who has lost a parent or someone close. I truly hope I can be of help, but I suppose really all you will be doing is helping that child to live with the loss, for no one ever gets over it.

So, when I thought about ways to help I pondered over what would potentially have helped me, not only at the time, but over the years. Surprisingly, or maybe not, many potential subjects in how a child might feel when dealing with the death of a parent came to light, including grief and mourning, changes in the family dynamic, guilt and blame, support systems, coping mechanisms and long term effects.

2

Grief and Mourning

This section will focus on the grief and mourning process, as well as how it can be affected by the age of the bereaved person. It will provide an overview of the stages of grief and how they can manifest differently in children. It will also discuss the importance of allowing bereaved children to experience their grief in their own way, and how to support them through it.

Grief is an inevitable and natural response to the loss of a loved one. It is an emotional and psychological process of adjusting to life without the person who has died. Grief is a complex and individual experience, and there is no one "right" way to grieve. The grieving process usually involves a combination of emotions, including sadness, guilt, anger, confusion, frustration, and despair. Grief can also involve physical symptoms, such as fatigue, difficulty concentrating, and changes in appetite. The stages of grief have been identified as denial, anger, bargaining, depression, and acceptance. Although these stages were originally identified in adults, they can also be observed in children. However, the stages may manifest differently in children than they do in adults, and grief in children can often be more complex. For children, grief can be especially difficult because they may not have the tools to process and express their emotions. It is important to allow children to experience their grief in their own way and on their own terms. This means allowing them to express their emotions, even if they seem irrational or overwhelming.

Grief and mourning is a complex and difficult process for anyone, especially children. A child of any age may have a difficult time understanding and expressing their feelings of sadness, loss, and confusion. They may not have the emotional maturity or vocabulary to express what they're going through and may also struggle with accepting that the parent is gone permanently. This can make it hard for them to communicate their feelings to others, making it difficult for them to receive the support they need.

Children at this age may also struggle with accepting that the parent is gone permanently. They may have a hard time accepting the reality of the death and may have difficulty letting go. They may also have trouble sleeping, eating, or concentrating on things they used to enjoy. They may have recurring nightmares or have difficulty trusting people. These symptoms are normal, but if they persist over time or become severe, it is important to seek professional help.

Children may also experience physical symptoms as a result of their grief. They may feel tired, have headaches, or stomach aches. They may also experience a loss of appetite or weight. These symptoms can be a sign that the child is struggling to cope with their loss and may need additional support.

It is also normal for some children to experience emotional outbursts and mood swings. They may become angry, irritable, or withdrawn. I have seen this in children who have lost someone, but it never happened with me, although I suppose I did become withdrawn, hiding in the shadows when it came time to discussing my family makeup. They may be more sensitive to criticism, or they may be more prone to crying. They may also feel guilty, blame themselves, or even blame others for their parent's death. These reactions are normal, but if they persist over time, it is important to give your child the love and support that they need before even thinking about seeking professional help. A little family love and understanding goes a long way and could even help the surviving parent and any siblings.

Overall, it's important to understand that grief is a normal and natural response to loss. It's important to provide support and understanding for a child who is grieving, and to help them find healthy ways to cope with their feelings. To me, what would have helped is for my mother and siblings to have spoken about it and not just filed it away. Family is important so even if the other parent is in no fit state to help, then a kind aunt or uncle is someone who should be welcomed to give it a try. Spending time with friends and family members who can provide emotional support is always the go to place in my books, or maybe even joining some sort of support group where you can get together with other families and just be there for each other. To me, therapy should be a last resort.

3

Changes in the Family Dynamic

When a parent dies, depending on the child's age, they may feel a sense of responsibility to "fill in" for the parent who is no longer there. They may feel like they need to take on additional responsibilities, such as cooking, cleaning, or helping to take care of siblings. This can be overwhelming and stressful for a child, and can cause feelings of confusion, abandonment, and insecurity.

If the remaining parent remarries or begins dating, the child may have difficulty adjusting to a new family structure. This can cause feelings of confusion, abandonment, and insecurity. They may feel like they are losing the parent all over again, or may feel resentful towards the new partner. They may also feel like they are being replaced, which can cause feelings of jealousy and insecurity.

The child may also feel guilty for wanting to move on and be happy again. They may feel like they are betraying their parent by enjoying activities or spending time with friends and family. This can be a difficult feeling to overcome and is where the simple act of talking about it can be a great help.

It's important to understand that these changes can be difficult for a child to navigate, and they may need extra support and understanding during this time. It is also important to keep in mind that every child will react differently and that it is okay for them to have their own feelings and reactions. It can be helpful to have open communication with the child, to listen and validate their feelings, and to provide reassurance that it is okay for them to feel a range of emotions during this difficult time.

It is also important to understand that healing is not a linear process, and that children may have good days and bad days. It's important to be patient and understanding, and to provide ongoing support as the child continues to grieve and adjust to the new family dynamic.

4

Guilt and Blame

Guilt and blame can be a common reaction for children who have lost a parent, particularly when they are young. Children may blame themselves for the parent's death, or may feel guilty for things they did or didn't do before the parent passed away. They may feel like they could have done something to prevent the death, or that they should have been able to save the parent. This can be a difficult feeling to overcome and can cause a lot of emotional pain.

Children may also blame others for their parent's death, such as medical professionals or even the other parent. They may feel angry or resentful towards them, and may have difficulty trusting them. This can be especially difficult if the child has a relationship with the person they are blaming.

These feelings of guilt and blame can be normal, but if they persist over time, it is important to talk about it and, if necessary, seek professional help. A therapist or counsellor can help the child work through these feelings and learn to cope with the loss in a healthy way. They can also help the child to understand that they are not responsible for the death and that it was not their fault.

It is also important for parents and other adults who are interacting with the child to be aware of their feelings and to validate them. The child needs to know that their feelings are normal and that they are not alone. It's also important to help the child understand that they are not responsible for what happened and that they did not cause the death.

Understanding that grief is a complex process and that everyone experiences it differently is an important factor. Children may have a harder time understanding and expressing their feelings of guilt and blame, so it is important to provide them with support and understanding during this difficult time.

5

Support Systems

Support systems are important for anyone going through a difficult time, including children who have lost a parent. It is important to help the child find healthy ways to cope with their grief, such as talking to a therapist or counsellor, joining a support group for children who have lost a parent, or spending time with friends and family members who can provide emotional support. The child may benefit from talking to someone who has gone through a similar experience, as well as someone who can provide practical advice and emotional support.

A therapist or counsellor can help the child

understand and cope with their feelings of grief and loss. They can also provide practical advice and emotional support, as well as help the child to develop healthy coping mechanisms, such as stress-management techniques or mindfulness practices.

Stress management techniques can be simple acts that a parent can assist with, one being to ensure that your child sleeps well. Sleep is essential for physical and emotional well-being, and keeps stress in check, with 9 to 12 hours of sleep a night being recommended for 6 to 12 year olds, and 8 to 10 hours a night for teenagers. Exercise, or some sort of physical activity, is an essential stress buster with 20 to 60 minutes recommended per day. So here is also a good time to bond with your child over your, and their, loss and run around or kick a ball together. I keep mentioning talking about it; something that my family never did. I have since found that talking about stressful situations with a trusted adult helps children put things in perspective and begin to heal. Setting some time aside for fun is also great family therapy. We all need time to do things that we enjoy, whether it is going to the beach as a family, watching a movie, listening to music or spending time with a hobby. Enjoy the great outdoors and just get outside. Did you know that some studies show that people who live in the country have less stress, depression and anxiety? So what are you waiting for? Finally, sometimes I found that writing about my feelings helped a great deal. I even wrote a few poems for my eyes only, but it helped.

Practising mindfulness produces many benefits for those going through stress and grief and, in my opinion, is better than an anti depressant!

Our minds are constantly active and we are always thinking of something. So, without complicating things too much you should encourage them to reduce their anxiety or depression by simply doing normal stuff. And when I say normal I mean colouring in a book, which, believe it or not, is a great way to get your child focused on a task. Going on a nature walk and encouraging your child to touch and feel the plants around them. Maybe even take a few photographs and get them to draw a picture later on. Even listening to music and focusing on the music and lyrics is a great activity. I am sure there are many more that you could think of which are relevant to you.

Joining a support group can also be beneficial for a child who has lost a parent. It can be helpful for the child to talk to others who have gone through a similar experience, as well as to receive support from those who understand what they are going through. Support groups can be a safe space for children to share their feelings and to learn from others who have gone through a similar thing in their life.

Spending time with friends and family members can also provide emotional support for a child who has lost a parent. They can provide a listening ear and a shoulder to cry on, as well as offer practical help and support. It's important to make sure that the child has a good support system in place, as it can be a vital factor in helping them to cope with their loss. Every child has a favourite aunt or uncle, so why not use that?

The main thing is that it is important to understand that grief is a normal and natural response to loss, and to provide support and understanding for a child who is grieving, and to help them find healthy ways to cope with their feelings is a priority. This *may* include therapy, joining a support group, or spending time with friends and family members who can provide emotional support. With the right support, the child can learn to cope with the loss in a healthy way. Personally I would always recommend the family route as they know you, and the child will feel more at ease.

6

Coping Mechanisms

Children may develop certain coping mechanisms to deal with their grief, when they have lost a parent, such as withdrawing from social activities or performing poorly in school. They may also begin to act out or display behavioural issues. These behaviours can be a sign that the child is struggling to cope with their loss and may need additional support.

It is important to be aware of these behaviours and provide support and understanding. A therapist or counsellor can help the child learn healthy coping mechanisms, but as a parent give it a go yourself first. Counsellors should be a last resort.

Withdrawing from social activities can be a sign that the child is struggling with feelings of sadness, anger, or guilt. They may not want to be around others or may not want to participate in activities that they used to enjoy. This can be a sign that the child is struggling to cope with their loss and may need additional support. In my case I was the opposite. All I had outside school was the Air Force Cadets so I ploughed everything I had in to that. I enjoyed cadets anyway and, even though I never told staff or cadets that my Dad had died, I think I just went to be with other people and to get out of the house, away from the lack of feeling or acknowledgement of my Dad's existence. It is interesting to note that the day of my Dad's funeral was a cadet night, and I still went to cadets. My Mum was obviously happy enough for me to go, as *I* was happy to be gone. It's funny though that I was sort of dying to tell someone when I was there, but I felt that if I did then they would feel sorry for me, when it was Dad who deserved those feelings. So, I suppose, in that sense I felt guilty if others cared about me. In any case if your child has a similar place to go please let them do it and don't give them the guilty feeling that they should be at home with everyone else.

Performing poorly in school can also be a sign that a child is struggling to cope with the loss of a parent. They may have difficulty concentrating, may have trouble completing assignments, or may have a decline in their grades. This can be a sign that the child is struggling to cope with the loss of a parent and may need additional support. In this instance talk to your child and perhaps even arrange a meeting with teaching staff for any help or additional instruction that is needed. Again, in my case, it was different, for my Dad died during the time when I was taking my final exams. Needless to say I failed them all, not because I didn't work hard but probably because, unconsciously, I just could not think straight.

Acting out or displaying behavioural issues can also be a sign that a child is struggling with the loss of a parent. They may become more argumentative, defiant, or aggressive. They may also have difficulty following rules or may display other problematic behaviours. This can be a sign that the child is struggling to cope with the loss of a parent and may need additional support. This was apparent in my 13 year old brother who became quite a rebel during his teenage years. I cannot help think that had my Dad been around he would have thought twice before doing any of the things that he did.

It is, therefore, necessary to be aware of these behaviours and provide support. A professional can help the child learn healthy coping mechanisms and strategies to manage their grief. In reality it is good to understand that these behaviours are normal reactions to a difficult and traumatic experience, and that with the right support, the child can learn to cope with the loss in a good way.

It's also vital to give children the space to grieve and the time to process their loss. Some coping mechanisms may take time to disappear or change, and forcing the child to change or stop them may be counter-productive.

7

Long Term Effects

Children who have lost a parent may experience long term effects, such as a difficulty forming close relationships, or trust issues. They may also have ongoing feelings of sadness, anger, or guilt. It is, therefore, important for the child to have ongoing support as they continue to grow and develop. As always the family should try to help, but remembering that a therapist or counsellor is another option if required.

Difficulty forming close relationships can be a serious long term effect of losing a parent. The child may have trouble trusting others or may be hesitant to get close to, or confide in, people. They may also have trouble forming close relationships with adults, such as teachers or other authority figures. This can be a sign that the child is still struggling to cope with their loss and may need additional support.

Ongoing feelings of sadness, anger, or guilt can also be long term effects of losing a parent. The child may have trouble coping with these feelings, even after a significant amount of time has passed. They may also have trouble dealing with anniversaries or other significant dates, such as birthdays or holidays.

I cannot stress too much how important a support system of friends and family really is. With the right support, the child can learn to cope with the loss and move forward in a healthy way.

Grief cannot be Ignored. People may experience grief in different ways. Children may have good days and bad days, and may experience different emotions at different stages of their life. In this light you must be understanding and supportive, to acknowledge the loss and accept their feelings.

As with me, if the parent had a terminal illness and the child had to watch them over a long period as they deteriorated the child's experience of grief and loss may be different from that of a child who has lost a parent suddenly. The child may have had the opportunity to say goodbye and to prepare for the loss, but they may also have had to endure a prolonged period of watching the parent's health decline. This can be a very difficult and traumatic experience for a child. The child may have feelings of sadness, anger, and guilt. They may have trouble coming to terms with the loss and may have difficulty accepting that the parent is gone. They may also have feelings of guilt, blame, or of helplessness, wishing that they could have done something to save their parent. In my case I couldn't say goodbye because my Dad did not know he was terminally ill. That made the whole situation more difficult for me, and it still is over 40 years later.

The child may have also developed a strong attachment to the parent during the time of their illness, as they have been able to spend more time with them, and may have taken on a caretaker role. This can make the loss even harder to bear. I had a lot of trouble adjusting to life without my Dad, and struggled to find meaning in my life without him. But, again, I had no one to talk to about it.

I cannot emphasize enough that the child has gone through a unique and difficult experience and that their grief process may be different from that of a child who has lost a parent suddenly. They may need additional support and understanding during this time. It's important for the child to have access to professional help, if required, to enable them to untangle and reconfigure their feelings, and provide them with coping mechanisms and strategies.

In all cases the provision of ongoing and meaningful support, is vital as they may continue to experience feelings of grief and loss as they grow and develop. With the right support, the child can learn to cope with the loss and move forward in a healthy way. If none of the family ever spoke of the death and just kept it bottled up inside, the child may have a harder time sorting out their grief and loss. In my personal experience a child must have the opportunity to talk about their feelings and to have their grief acknowledged. When families don't talk about the death, children may feel like they are not allowed to grieve or that their feelings are not important. This can make it harder for them to come to terms with the loss and to cope with their grief in a healthy way. Indeed when I was still living at home I felt that I couldn't show any weakness, so took my feelings to my bedroom until they subsided.

Because I was not able to discuss my grief, I kept my feelings inside me, a fact which has probably led to unseen long term emotional and psychological effects. I was always quite shy anyway but I definitely became more withdrawn, and anxious, and I strongly believe that my grief, coupled with being in a loveless relationship when I was older, led to depression; which I just couldn't shake. Some people may have trouble trusting others or may have difficulty forming close relationships. They may also have trouble adjusting to life without the parent, and may struggle to find meaning in their life without them. I think I just felt lonely and actively sought out someone to love and who loved me, resulting in me latching on to the first person who cared; the wrong person as it transpired, which didn't end well, but did have the knock on effect of me waking up to my grief.

Families, as difficult as it may seem, must be able to have open and honest conversations about the death, to allow the child to express their feelings, and to provide them with love, support and understanding. Counsellors can be helpful in this situation, as they can provide a safe space for the child to talk about their feelings and to process their grief. They can also help the child understand that it is normal for them to have sad and regretful feelings, and that is really is okay to grieve the loss of these experiences with their parent. Professionals can also provide strategies for coping with these feelings and emotions and help the child to explore and find ways to honour their parent's memory, and to include them in their special life events in some way. Additionally the counsellor can help the child work through their feelings and provide support as they navigate the grief process. Don't forget, the family is a ready-made counsellor, so with the help of loved ones the child can learn to cope with their feelings of regret, loss and sadness, and find a new sense of normalcy in their life.

If the child is now an adult and still thinks of their dead parent on a daily basis, it may indicate that they have not fully processed their grief and loss. Grief is a complex and personal process, and it can take different amounts of time for people to work through it. It's not uncommon for people to continue to think about and miss their loved ones, even years after their death. I am a prime example.

It is normal for the adult child to continue to think about and miss their parent. It doesn't mean they haven't moved on, just that they have come to terms with their loss, and realise that the situation is out of their control. Again, they may need additional support and understanding as they continue to process their grief. Finding ways to cope with their grief and remember their parent is important too. They may find comfort in writing, art, music, or other forms of expression. They may also find it helpful to volunteer, to travel, or to engage in other activities that give them a sense of purpose and fulfilment. For me I had always idolised my father. He was a soldier, and that is all I ever wanted to be. So I did, and made sure that I was a soldier he could be proud of, eventually becoming an Officer.

In the end grief is not something that can be "gotten over" or "finished", it will always be a part of you. You may have good days and bad days, but it is important for you to have patience and understanding towards yourself. The adult child should not put pressure on themselves to "get over" the loss or to "move on" quickly. Grief is a lifelong process that takes time and effort. They should allow themselves to grieve in their own way and in their own time, and understand that the memories, emotions, and feelings associated with their parent will change and evolve over time, and that it is alright to have different feelings at different stages of their life. They may also have triggers that bring up feelings of grief, and it's important for them to be prepared for those.

8

The Reality of Loss

If the first dead body that the child ever saw was that of their parent, the experience can be particularly traumatic and difficult for them to cope with. The child may have difficulty understanding the finality of death and may have difficulty accepting that their parent is gone. They may also have trouble with the physical reality of death, as they most likely would have never seen a dead body before. I have to say that being forced to view my Dad's body has had a lasting impact on me, but not in a bad way. Although I never said it, I never in my own mind forgave my mother for putting us through it. However, in a way I am glad that I saw him, because the funeral director had done a great job in making my gravely ill father look good, and outwardly at least, be the man I knew and loved. So for that I will always be thankful.

If the first funeral that the child ever went to was that of their parent, the experience can be particularly difficult for them to comprehend. Funerals can be difficult for adults to understand and cope with, let alone children.

I keep harping on about family support, but ongoing support is so very important, as they may continue to experience feelings of grief and loss as they grow and develop. With family love and support, the child can learn to cope with the loss and move forward in a good way.

Some of the things that can be done to help the child cope with the funeral are:

Give them age-appropriate explanations and answer their questions honestly. Prepare them for what they will see and experience at the funeral. Allow them to participate in the funeral service in a way that feels comfortable for them. Give them the opportunity to say goodbye to the deceased parent in their own way. Encourage them to talk about their feelings, and let them know that their feelings are normal and valid. Be patient and understanding and let them know that you are there for them.

Needless to say, I had none of this.

It *can* be beneficial for a child to talk about their feelings of grief and loss with a family member or friend. So please at least try. Again, it is important for children to have the opportunity to express their feelings and to have their grief acknowledged. Having someone to talk to can provide a sense of emotional support and understanding for the child. A family member or friend can also provide practical advice, and can help the child to cope with their feelings. It's important for the family member or friend to be a good listener, to validate the child's feelings, and to provide them with a safe space to express their emotions. They should also be willing to answer any questions the child may have, and to provide them with accurate information about the death.

It's also important to note that while talking with a family member or friend can be beneficial, it's not a substitute for professional help.

In the end grief is a personal and unique

experience, and everyone deals with it differently. Feelings of shock, confusion, disbelief, anger, guilt, and despair are normal. Some children may find talking about their grief helpful, while others may prefer not to talk about it. So please respect the child's needs and preferences, and provide them with the support that they require. In the case of an adult child it is normal for them to experience feelings of regret and sadness that the deceased parent never got to see important life events such as the child's marriage or the birth of their own children. I certainly have these feelings. Such feelings can be especially strong when the child is faced with these milestones or when they are around others who have *their* parents present at these events. These feelings can be particularly difficult to cope with, as they may be accompanied by a sense of loss and longing for the parent who is no longer there to share in these special moments. The adult child may also feel guilty for not having been able to share these experiences with their parent. A great way to honour a deceased parent is to include them in special events, for example displaying their photo at a wedding ceremony.

9

My Advice

I have seen death and experienced grief as both a child and an adult, and it is not a good thing, but unfortunately it does come to us all at some stage in our lives. My advice to you as a parent or care giver is first to take the time to acknowledge and accept your own feelings, for to be in the position of trying to help a child deal with loss, you must have dealt with it too. So, please, allow *yourself* to cry, express your own feelings through writing about it, or talking to a friend or relative. Find ways to remember your loved one through pictures, videos, or other items that help keep their memory alive. It may sound strange but I often found myself in the attic cuddling and sniffing my Dad's clothes; but it helped. It is normal to feel a strong connection to a loved one who has passed away, and to want to find ways to feel close to them. Everyone grieves differently, and there is no right or wrong way to cope with loss. It is important to find healthy and constructive ways to express your emotions and to remember your loved one in meaningful ways.

Reaching out to family and friends who can provide emotional and practical support is always a good thing. This can help to reduce the sense of isolation that often accompanies grief. Above all, take care of yourself; your physical and emotional needs. Make sure to get enough sleep, eat healthy, and exercise. Do activities that bring you joy and provide a distraction from your grief. Obviously there is no timeline for this, but it will be surprisingly quick and will most likely occur in the time leading up to the funeral. Naturally you will need to be the brave one. Talk to your children about death. It can be a difficult task, but it is important to discuss death in a manner which is easily understood, and to be honest. Give children the opportunity to ask questions and express their feelings; don't sweep it under the carpet like my mother did. If needed, seek professional help from a mental health professional.

It is important to reach out to family and friends during periods of grief. Talking to someone who is supportive and understanding can help you cope with the emotions and thoughts associated with grief. Taking care of your physical health, and that of your children, is an important priority. Eating a balanced and healthy diet, exercising regularly, and getting enough sleep are essential for your physical and mental health. Refusing to eat or look after yourself never did anyone any good. Try to maintain a regular routine as much as possible. Above all, take time to heal. Spend time alone or with loved ones doing activities that bring you comfort and joy. Listen to music, read a book, watch a movie, or take a walk in the park. Encourage your bereaved children to play outside with their friends or cousins. It is normal to experience a wide range of emotions during times of grief. Allow yourself and your kids to feel and express your emotions in a healthy way. Practice self-compassion. Be kind to yourself during this difficult time. It is okay to take time for yourself and to make mistakes. Acceptance and understanding of your circumstances is essential. If you feel overwhelmed or unable to cope with your grief, seeking professional help *is* important, so forget about any stigmas that you may feel.

In most cases terminal illness is out in the open from day one, so it is important for a child who knows their parent is terminally ill to have a supportive network of friends and family to talk to about their thoughts and feelings. This can help them process the situation and understand what is happening. It can also be helpful to have a therapist of some sort available to provide emotional support and guidance. When the parent is nearing death, it can be helpful to create rituals or memorable experiences to share with their parent. Have a chat, have a laugh. It all helps, believe me. These moments can help the child find closure and create lasting memories. After the death, it is important to acknowledge and honour the parent's life and not just sweep them under the carpet. This can include attending a memorial service, writing a letter to them, or creating a memory book of their life.

It is also important to find ways to remember the parent, such as looking at photos or visiting places they used to go to. It is normal to experience a range of emotions during and after the death of a parent, and it is important to find ways to express those feelings. Talking to a trusted friend or family member can provide comfort during this time. It can also be beneficial to take part in activities that honour the parent's memory, such as taking part in a charity event or volunteering your time.

From my experience it can be very difficult to deal with the death of a parent when no one talks about it, but it is important to remember that it is *okay* to talk about it and to share your feelings with those who may be able to help you.

Illness and death is an incredibly difficult situation for any child to deal with, and there is no one-size-fits-all answer. It is important to remember that every child deals with grief differently, and you should be patient and understanding with them. The first step is to give the child the space to grieve. Allow them to express their sadness in whatever way they need to. Offer a listening ear, be available to talk, be patient and understanding, cry, or take part in activities to remember the lost parent. It can also be helpful to encourage the child to talk about their parent and their memories together; positive and happy memories. Reassure the child that they are loved and that their feelings are normal. Share stories and memories of the parent, look at old photos, and celebrate special occasions in their memory. Smile if you can.

It is completely understandable for me to still think of my Dad and to cry after over 40 years. Grief is a process that does not have a timeline. Don't be afraid of it. Honour your feelings and take care of yourself and your children. But, above all, please remember that it is good to talk.

ABOUT THE AUTHOR

Jack Mallory has not only worked in the field of coaching and personal development mentoring, but also draws upon his years of life experience in his desire to help others learn from their own mistakes, and those of others, in order that they may have what we all desire; a happy and fulfilling life.

OTHER BOOKS BY THIS AUTHOR

Ditch the Git.......before it's too late! - How to spot and escape a bad relationship before it starts.

The Pocket Guide to Good Parenting.

www.ingramcontent.com/pod-product-compliance
Lightning Source LLC
Chambersburg PA
CBHW070312010526
44107CB00056B/2569